FROM
NOW ON

How To Bring Your Vision To Life

Chanel Prabatah

First paperback edition June 2024

ISBN 979-8-9908045-0-0 (paperback)

ISBN 979-8-9908045-1-7 (ebook)

Published by Embodied Spirals

Contents

Dedication

To my ancestors,

Thank you for holding me up on your shoulders.

Introduction

When I first embarked on this journey to write this book, I really put the pressure on myself to write something that was worthy to be next to best selling books that contained thousand upon thousands of words. I was going against the creative process and allowing my ego to get the best of me because I thought I only needed to check things off of a list. As long as I stayed on "task", I would get the results I wanted.

However, this process has been far from the cookie cutter format I had in my mind. From having the idea to write a book 5 years ago to toiling with the topic to then having a baby and postponing the whole process. To make matters worse, I felt like I had to share with others what I was doing because I felt stagnant just working a 9 to 5 job and kept saying I was writing a book when the whole time I was just happy with the idea of it and not the execution part. Then I punished myself every time someone asked me about it and I was still in the same place I was months ago.

I knew deep in my heart I was meant to share my insight through storytelling but my mental blocks were holding me back. I thought I had to be a certain way to be an author but I just needed to express myself through my words. Countless times I've heard someone tell me my words provided them with comfort and reassurance, but here I was unable to give it to myself when I needed it the most.

You ever heard of the wounded healer? Well that's how I felt. I could see the bigger picture for others but not for myself and it really perplexed me. I ended up realizing that I was too hyper focused on the book and needed to take a break to see things differently.

I had to live life from a different vantage point. I had to feel my emotions instead of ignoring them. That consisted of me crying my eyes out, detaching myself from the world I knew, and taking a trip inward. Was it an easy task? Definitely not, but it was necessary for me to produce this book you have today.

Meditation was the key to my shift. It truly gave me the answers I was searching for and it taught me how to trust my intuition. I was running away from this book because I didn't think I could do it on my own. However, that was a belief I had to eliminate.

I know you've heard someone say, "From now on, I'm going to do such and such," but how do you put that into action? *From Now On* is a reminder to rediscover the forgotten parts of yourself.

We're going to take a journey. First, we're going to the past to get some key ingredients that will inspire our present moment. Then, we'll decide how we want to put these ingredients together to create future "now" moments, full of wonder and awe.

May this book encourage you to believe in your gifts, and express them fully as you continue to unfold.

Once Upon A Time

Blank Canvas

When we come into this world, we're void of any impressions, opinions, or preferences. Before our arrival, we are floating in warm water with all our needs being met. After our birth, we are shocked to be breathing air in a loud, cold, and uncomfortable environment. We cry to get the attention of our parents when we are hungry or need our diaper changed. During infancy, we are instinctively in survival mode and want to be as comfortable as possible. We want to keep our bellies full, have a dry diaper and be snuggly warm.

The surface of our canvas is primed by our parents. This is the point where our attachment style develops. The most common styles are secure, anxious and avoidant. A secure baby knows when he or she cries that their needs will be met promptly. An anxious baby is prone to clinging more to their parents for fear of their parents not returning. On the other hand, an avoidant baby is less likely to pay attention to their parents and doesn't seek comfort from them. This sets the stage for future relationships but the attachment style can change overtime.

Eventually our engagement with family, friends and others in our community establishes the background of our canvas. As time progresses, we begin to learn through the exploration of our world. We learn how to behave by observing the adults in our environment. Whether the behavior is deemed good or bad has no bearing on us because we don't know the difference. We eventually learn what's acceptable behavior by our parents' reaction. At this stage, everything is being imposed on us because we don't have a clear understanding of the world yet.

Introspection

However, there comes a point in our life when we have to address the person we became. The way to this awareness is by going deep within ourselves but that can be nerve-racking when we've ignored things for so long. Yet, the only way to reach the next level in our lives is by doing so. We have to start examining how we feel about ourselves, why we react the way we do, and where it all originated from.

At this point, that blank canvas has turned into a portrait brimming with colors. We are evolving works of art and the beauty is that we can alter our colors whenever we want. We may have forgotten but we always have the ability to change.

So let's talk about your feelings about yourself. Do you feel good about the person you are today? When it comes to your vision, do you believe it's possible for you? Do you believe you deserve the desires of your heart? The reality is that if you don't believe you are worthy of your desires, there is no way for it to come into your life.

Your beliefs, which are repeated thoughts in your mind, have to be in alignment with the way YOU want your life to be. The difference between wanting something versus actually having it is a shift in your perspective. The law of vibration states that every thought has its own unique frequency. So doubt and belief can't be vibrating at the same level. You can't expect to get the results of belief when you're full of doubt.

But the beautiful thing about being human is that we have the ability to change by thought alone. Of course, it will take some time for the old thought patterns to end fully but it's still doable to continue reinforcing the new thoughts.

Now, let's talk about the way you react to life. Who did you see responding the same way as you do to things? Are you reacting from a place of your childhood fears and traumas like a dark cloud that won't ever go away? These are the type of questions you have to explore to understand yourself on a deeper level.

Let's talk about a topic that affects us all: money. How do you respond to it? Are you afraid to spend it due to a scarcity mindset? Or do you squander it because you don't feel worthy enough to keep it in your possession? We can trace our money habits back to our childhood. And that's just talking about money. Imagine the other topics we can dive into like health, love, career, and spirituality. Once we're honest with ourselves, we can be aware of what's happening in our lives and discontinue being on autopilot.

Our subconscious mind reveals these things to our awareness to help us discern where we need to make adjustments. This brings me to someone you may have forgotten about: your inner child. The inner child encompasses all the younger versions of yourself that remain within you. And the smaller you's are still seeking the things you desired as a child.

Let's take it a step further. How do you describe your soul? Do you remember yourself when you were 5 years old? What about 15 years old? 25 years old? Your body may have changed but the essence peering through your beautiful eyes didn't. That's your soul. The reality is that we are all God, just combined in different ways.

Inner Child Worthiness

Before we lay our past to rest, let's spend some time with our inner child. This is when we get to acknowledge joyful moments from our childhood and give ourselves a chance to explore things we wanted to do as a child. This could be something as simple as going to a space center, horseback riding, tap dancing, or painting.

A gentle reminder: please do NOT judge or psych yourself out of trying something new due to your age. Nothing is out of your reach beloved. You are full of life; so why not explore it without limits. Also, don't believe the "hype" of following a certain timeline; there isn't one. Be kind to yourself and allow yourself to be wild; free of constraints.

I'm writing this as my kids are holding hands and swinging around laughing. Can you imagine doing that with someone you love? Just because we're adults doesn't mean we can't have a childlike spirit. Sometimes we get too serious as adults and miss out on opportunities to laugh and have fun. It's time to embrace life.

Your inner child is your higher self; When you were born you were the closest to God because your spirit just transitioned from the spiritual realm to the physical one. So the wisdom and guidance you need is still within you. However, you have to take the time to tap into your spirit.

We think someone is going to come save us but no one is coming. The change you want is on the other side of your inspired action and if you don't change in anyway, nothing in your life will change. You have the potential but if you never act on it, guess what? It'll be just that: potential.

I remember a time in my life when I thought my life would magically change on it's own because I had all these amazing ideas in my mind. However, I didn't take any action and you know what happened? Nothing. It wasn't until I took inspired action and moved outside of my comfort zone that my life started to shift for the better.

You have to trust your intuition. No one knows what's best for you but yourself. You have to trust your first mind like the older generations around me would say. Don't overthink things; trust that you are being guided towards the best experiences for your highest good.

Of course, we're humans and want to know what's going to happen beforehand but that's not how God works. Imagine if God revealed everything that's going to happen in your life; could you really handle the good, the bad, and the ugly? You would probably be debilitated by the challenging stuff. That's why we receive nuggets of information and as we follow our internal guidance, more is, subsequently, revealed to us. If you never take the first step, you'll never reach the tenth one.

Flowing with your inner child allows you to move freely towards experiences that are naturally enjoyable to you. Society teaches us that success only comes from struggling and doing things we don't like but that's not the truth. You can follow what piques your interest and create from that vantage point. Now, I'm not saying you're going to be absolved of all challenges but at least you'll be doing something that you find pleasure in.

We all have different experiences and that allows us to bring something unique to the table. So lean towards the things that are natural and effortless to you. And don't tell me: "I don't have a purpose" or "I don't know what to do with myself". Everyone has gifts and you have to give yourself permission to move freely to discover yours.

"Life" will always have something going on but you can't let that stop you from living in your purpose. God has people waiting on you to share your gifts and the way you express yourself is going to inspire them to do the same. You are that important and quite frankly, the gifts you are hiding, are not yours! They are there to encourage others to shine their light brighter.

Here & Now

Detach

As you understand more about yourself, there comes a point in time where you have to detach yourself from everything that doesn't serve your highest good. The reality is that we have to die to it all if we want to reach the next step in our journey. For example, look at how trees go through different stages. In the wintertime, they are dormant which is their death. During the spring time, it's their rebirth. While their growth is during the summertime and they bear fruit during the fall time. Even though the tree is "alive" the entire time, it still surrenders to the cycle of death and rebirth every year. We are a part of nature so the same is true for us. The problem is when we get stuck in one period, instead of allowing the cycle to proceed.

Just like when a loved one passes away, we are in a state of denial. I remember when my beloved Grandpa passed away; it just didn't seem real to me and I was waiting for him to walk through the front door but it never happened. Denial can sound like, "Well I'm just that way and I can't change it." Do you know how false, yet true that statement is? The reality is that life will always reveal what we think is true to us.

Whenever you are being limited, gently remind yourself of what you do want in your life. Remember to affirm yourself in the present tense even if your reality doesn't reflect that. For instance, saying something in the future tense is like dangling a carrot in front you; always out of your reach.

The cycle of obtaining and releasing will continue to transpire if we will allow ourselves to be fully immersed in God. You may even become angry because you feel like you shouldn't have to continue releasing yourself from people, places, and things you once loved dearly. However, there is so much available to us when we surrender to these spiritual and emotional deaths. We get so hung up on the physical death that we forget about the other ones we experience throughout our lives. And to be quite honest, it's ok to feel angry or any similar emotions but you can't get stuck there.

After allowing yourself to feel, there comes a point in time where you try to bargain with the process and not fully commit yourself to it. I like to think of it as riding the fence or having one foot in and the other one out. The mind, better known as the ego, will do anything it can to keep you "safe" but it's really an illusion. I understand the known is familiar to you but is it really benefiting you?

Just like a loved one passing away, we get to a point of intense grief and depression. The same experience happens when you let go of everything you know, to surrender to the unknown. There's been a few times in my life where I was sobbing my eyes out because I chose to release everything I knew, to transcend to the next level in my life.

To aid with this process, you can meditate and utilize tapping. Meditation allows you to connect with God. Prayer is you talking to God and meditation is God talking back to you. Of course, it's easier to pray but meditation is worthwhile. In terms of meditating, give yourself time to move pass your restless mind and be able to sit in the seat of your soul. Just like any other practice, you have to apply yourself to it to see results.

Tapping is another method of releasing trapped emotions stuck inside of your body. What you do is tap certain points on your body and repeat different phrases to release unwanted thoughts and feelings. There are books, videos and even apps that do guided tapping sessions. Just do a simple search online and find what appeals to you.

Now it's time to enrich your life with nurturing words. Saying affirmations in the mirror is an easy way to accomplish this. Affirmations are thoughts we think and words we speak. So it's time to use them to our benefit.

You know how the eyes are the windows to our soul. Well that's the reason why were getting in the mirror so we can speak directly to ourselves. When I first started mirror work years ago, it was very awkward for me to speak kindly to myself. Most of the time when we look at ourselves in the mirror, we're berating ourselves and looking at all of our "imperfections".

Also, the things I was saying to myself were the things I wanted to hear from my parents. You see how all of this is tying together. We are literally healing our inner child. We are giving them the confidence to live life NOW and not in some far away place called the future.

You want to have a couple affirmations that reflect what you desire in your life. I suggest starting with something simple like, "I love you, your name." The main thing to remember when formulating your affirmations is placing them in the present tense. The future isn't here and the past is gone. So make sure you do that to magnetize your affirmations into your reality, even if it isn't happening yet. I used to boast about "keeping it real" and felt like saying stuff that wasn't present in my reality was lying. But what you say now becomes your future moments.

To do mirror work, go stand in front of a mirror. Even using a handheld mirror or pulling the mirror down from inside your car is perfectly fine. It's time to look into those beautiful eyes and speak kindly to yourself. Make sure you say your affirmations aloud while looking into your eyes. The more enthusiasm and feelings you have behind your affirmations, the faster you will bring your beliefs into fruition. In the beginning, it is very weird to talk to yourself but overtime, you will get used to it. Even when you doubt it, keep applying yourself to it day in and day out.

For example, I like to say my affirmations in the bathroom mirror and play music afterwards that really gets me into a good mood. I start clapping and even singing loudly. You really have to border the line of insanity to convince yourself that you are worthy of the things you are speaking into existence.

You are bringing something from the unseen to the seen. You come from the Creator so you possess the capabilities of the One who created you. That is truly a wonderful thing to know. You have to see what you want in your mind's eye before it reveals itself in the physical realm. Trust the process and remember that staying open allows God to bring what we want the best way to us.

What Do I Want Right Now?

When it comes to your vision, you have to get crystal clear about what you want in your life. How many times have you asked someone what they want and their response was all the things they didn't want? The truth is these people do know what they want because it's the opposite of what they don't want.

Unfortunately, our society thrives on people paying attention to negative things. Just turn on the news and you'll hear a plethora of stories that bring on fear. It's meant to keep you paranoid so you don't make any traction in your life. Despite that, you can't let it derail you from going after what you want in your life.

So grab a blue pen and white paper to brainstorm different possibilities for yourself. Write down every option that crosses your mind even the ones that seem far-fetched. Then go over each item and ask yourself why you want this? Sometimes we think we want a particular thing or experience just for the sake of it but it usually points to something deeper. So dive deep my friend.

In a world where people are "busy" and put off their dreams because of "life", you want to put your energy towards your vision by keeping it in the forefront of your mind. Now that doesn't mean you don't take care of your responsibilities but it does mean make it a point to complete even a little task towards your vision each day. It's easier to implement one new thing to your life versus multiples ones at a time.

Furthermore, tending to one task at a time helps builds your confidence and it will eventually become second nature to you. When something becomes instinctive, it helps you move forward when the going gets tough.

Let's talk about the snowball effect. Basically, there is a small snowball rolling down a hill and becomes larger by the time it lands at the foot of the hill. So let's think of it in terms of your vision: you start off with something doable and as you progress, it will eventually take on a life of its own.

For example, I'm a disciplined person but I procrastinate on stuff that frightens me. My fear had me scared to write this book for over 5 years. I signed up for a writing mentorship but I kept avoiding the process. It wasn't until I listened to my mentor's advice and created measurable steps to help me create this book. I was able to write my outline, which is 10% of the book, within 15 days. Mind you, I was "trying" to write this book after being in the mentorship over a year and a half. I can hear my mentor, saying "Give yourself grace." The good news is that after I applied myself, I was able to go from having nothing to having a whole outline and 3 chapters done in less than a month.

Remember you aren't the first person trying to do something and you won't be the last so find inspiration from others. They can guide you along your journey. Even if what you're going after is out the "ordinary", you can still use someone's experience as a guide. We have the world at our fingertips via smartphones; so it's even easier to find information we need. YouTube is a good resource to use because there is so many videos available. The great thing is that you get to see how things are done. Remember let these resources work for you and not the other way around. Yes, entertainment is available but don't let the time slip by you because you got distracted.

Another resource is the library because of the different resources available. Books are a wealth of knowledge and you can't find a better place to find information. Taking time to divulge in a book can be the reason you connect the dots to your vision. Also, the library offers movies, clubs and different events that can be of interest to you. I've never been a fan of the library but as an adult, I've opened myself to it and am enjoying what my local library offers.

Change Is The Only Constant

The only thing that remains the same is change. Picture this: if you stepped into a river today and went back tomorrow, it would not be the same water from yesterday. Nothing is ever the same even if it "looks" like it. Nature may have rivers and forests that look the same but if we really look at it, we'd see that it is shifting and constantly changing. Take our bodies, for instance. Is your body still the same from when you were a newborn, a child, an adolescent or an adult? Of course not. Even as an adult, our body continues to change. So, how could one expect life to remain the same when our bodies don't even do that?

We're always changing: for better or for worse. So which path are you going to take? Going with the flow as things present themselves is going to make life much easier to handle. We have to be comfortable in the unknownness and trust that life is really working out for our highest good. Have some faith and keep at it. Don't let go of your vision regardless of what you see in your reality because it doesn't matter.

Here's an example I like to use for going with the flow. Let's say you are in a river holding on to the bank because you want to control everything around you. The speed of the river and how the fish are swimming is causing discord in you but the truth is you're afraid to accept the river as it is. So what do you think happens next? Nothing because you haven't released your grip to move. Finally, you muster the courage to let go and you realize you can maneuver around boulders and pick different routes along the way.

In the past, I've tried to control every aspect of my life but was upset when I didn't get the results I wanted. My stronghold on having control was a response from my childhood because I needed to have a predictable result. And if we take it a step further, the truth is that control is really another form of fear. The fear of being hurt, the fear of not getting what we deserve or even the fear of being wildly successful.

As we all know, we will never control everything around us and trying to do so will only cause more discord in our lives. We have to be ok surrendering to the present moment and not worrying so much about our future. God's timing is better than ours.

Have you ever wanted something so badly and when you finally got it, it wasn't as perked up as you thought it would be? You might think you really want something but it may not be what's best for you. If we look back on our lives, every person can recall a time we were stuck on something or someone. We might have even tried to force things but for whatever reason it still didn't work out. And you know what, I bet we're thankful it didn't now that we're at a different place in our lives.

In addition, I know certain moments in our life were amazing and we want to relish in them forever but that's coming from a scarcity mindset. If you want to stay in a moment forever, it's like you're proclaiming that you're not going to get any other moments similar to that in the future. Whatever you focus on, you'll get more of that and I'm speaking from experience.

I know you're probably like, "So, you never paid attention to problems in your life?" The truth is I was trying to be problem solver of the year and it only perpetuated the same issues. It wasn't until I said enough is enough and made a conscious effort to look at the circumstances in my life differently.

I stopped reacting to the things like it was the end of the world. Also, I made it a point to conserve my energy, stop trying to solve everyone else's problems and have some good boundaries for myself. Did this happen overnight? Of course not but I became very intentional with my life.

That's why we should be conscious of what we are digesting on a daily basis. Start paying attention to your thoughts when you first wake up in the morning. How you are feeling? What type of foods are you eating? How are you speaking to yourself when you walk past the mirror? How are you referring to your children and spouse? How do you feel about your job and your day to day life?

How are the majority of your conversations during the course of a day? What are you watching on television? What are you looking at on social media? Are you feeling bad because of someone else's life or are you looking at things that bring you fulfillment and joy? We don't think about this all the time but we should be intentional with everything we do. This can look like the way you walk, talk, how you prepare your food, move your body and express yourself authenticity.

I'm going to give you a great example of how I learned how to surrender. A couple years ago, I surprised my husband with skydiving for his birthday. We are thrill seekers and enjoy adventures so I booked it for both of us. We got strapped up and my nerves started getting to me. Then, it was time to get on the plane and I hear the pilot say, "The engine isn't turning on," and I was thinking "Oh boy. What did I get us into?!" But the pilot said it was doing that because the plane wasn't being used during the week, only on the weekends.

Other people started getting on the plane like professional skydivers and people doing tandem rides. So we're elevating into the sky and I'm getting super nervous like why did I choose this? Mind you, I had already jumped out of the Stratosphere Hotel in Las Vegas, but here I was freaking out. So the light goes off for a guy to tandem jump at 9,000 feet. They open the door and he just zips out so fast that I really started going crazy inside.

We finally reach our level of 13,000 feet and the professionals jump out first including one group holding hands in a circle. The guys attached to me and my husband asked who was going to go first and my husband said, "Ladies first". Talk about a gentleman. Haha. Anyways, here I was standing at the edge of this open plane and the man told me he'd push us out.

All I could do was surrender to the moment, as I fell out of that plane screaming profusely. The wind was whipping in my face and I had to remember to get my face together because the guy was recording me.

I thought I was going to have the same sensation as riding a rollercoaster and jumping out of the Stratosphere, but it was different. It felt like a weightless fall until you got closer to the Earth. And to think, my imagination had me thinking I was going to have a bad experience when it was quite the opposite.

Please be careful how you use your imagination. It can either work for you or against you.

The Internal World

Have you ever paid attention to your thoughts? Society tries to convince us that it's normal to talk negatively to ourselves because we're exposed to it on a daily basis. However, we can't embody that way of living. It will never bring the desires of our heart to us.

We have to be kinder to ourselves. Would you belittle a child or a friend for a small mistake? Or call them out of their name because of how they look? Of course not. So why would you do it to yourself?

And I'm preaching to myself because I was just being self conscious about wearing a sports bra and leggings to an appointment because I was fixated on my stomach. Mind you, I've given birth to three beautiful children. My mind perceives my body as one way while it's actually another way. That's why we have to pay attention to what we are thinking and speaking to ourselves.

Did you know when you talk to water it takes on the vibration of the words spoken? They've done studies where they speak either positive or negative words to water. Then they do a process to freeze and exam the ice under a microscope to reveal different patterns. The positive words resulted in beautiful designs while the negative ones resulted in erratic shapes.

Now let's take it a step further. Our bodies consist of over 60% water and our brains are over 75% water. All of our cells hear and feel every thought and emotion we're having on a daily basis; while it's just trying to keep us healthy   and   alive. Can you imagine what type of environment we're creating for our organs when we bellyache all the time versus speaking more kindly to ourselves? The environments are going to be totally different; one is going to promote health while the other is going to be prone to disease.

On a daily basis, we should be observing our thoughts. If you catch yourself complaining or talking ill of yourself, realize what you're doing, acknowledge it and alter it to a helpful thought instead. For instance, if you walk past a mirror and judge yourself. Change that thought immediately and say "I forgive myself for being so judgmental of my being. I'm thankful to have a fully functioning body that takes care of me. I am a work in progress and I love all of me." Just because you are dissatisfied with something doesn't mean you go hard on yourself. Be aware of what you don't like and do something about it.

Also, being kind to yourself doesn't mean you're being delusional. It actually gives you the courage to walk into the unknown. And with that confidence, it will allow you to be open to trying new things.

What you see right now is a result from your past actions and thoughts. To see something different in your reality, you have to modify your thoughts and actions to create new future "now" moments. I know it's a little trippy but time is all connected and really the same. So the only time to make changes and move differently is now.

From Now On

Inspired Action

Taking inspired action is important to bring your vision to life. This looks like taking action outside of your familiarity and being ok trying new things for the first time. In the past, I wanted to know all the details before taking any action, but life doesn't work that way. To be honest, I was moving out of fear because I wanted to make sure I didn't "fail". Nothing is really a failure especially when you take the time to understand the lesson behind your attempt.

Many of us have been raised to find fault in everything and think of every excuse why something won't work. Just as you can pay attention to what can go wrong, you can shift that perspective and focus on what can go right.

I came across this affirmation: I move forward even when facing fear. Fear is supposed to protect us from danger. In the past, our ancestors were dealing with predators trying to attack them; so fear was advantageous. However, we know how fear can debilitate us from doing anything even if it's beneficial for us. Take those risks and trust that your ancestors are also guiding you on your journey.

I saw a quote that stated, "You can't expect front row seats when you've given nose bleed efforts." You're not going to get something for nothing. Just like the saying you reap what you sow. You have the power to change your life and more importantly, you can do it. Believe in yourself and put in the work. Do the research, speak to others doing what you want and hold yourself accountable.

Also, please don't consume yourself with the whole process and freeze up. Instead, figure out what you can do today to bring you one step closer to your vision. The time is going by anyways; so, why not make the most of it.

You have to put yourself in a position to "succeed" and I use this terminology loosely because failure and success are a shift in perspective. As I stated before, many are afraid to try new things out of fear of failing but the only way you're going to discover something different is by trying it.

And yes, you may fail at your first attempt, but you also obtained a valuable lesson. I remember reading that Thomas Edison tried creating the light bulb over 10,000 times. He said he didn't fail but found 10,000 ways it wouldn't work. A mental shift will either convince you to quit or give it another chance.

We may not know it at the time but everything we do is working out for our highest good even if it makes no sense at the time. For instance, when I was in college, I had my sights on becoming an attorney. I worked at a few law firms, got in touch with the law school connected to my university and took the LSAT twice. However, I only applied to one law school and ended up moving to California because I didn't get accepted. And for the longest time, it bothered me because I didn't follow through with my dream, but as I observed the attorneys I worked with, it made me realize that they had more constraints than I desired.

A few years later, I ended up becoming a judicial assistant and my law experience helped me be successful in that position. You might think you wasted time doing something in your past, but it gave you the edge to express yourself differently.

When we can be honest about our efforts, we can move in a better manner. Most times people get upset when they don't have what they want, but have they done the work?Some blame others for their problems like their parents and the environment they grew up in. But as adults we have to hold ourselves accountable for the life we are currently living.

Self-Preservation

I really want you to spend time with yourself. Many people like to distract themselves with cell phones, laptops, television and even other people. But when you have the courage to tap into your inner being, what a world of a difference your life can be. Spending time with yourself helps you follow your heart and brings more clarity to your vision.

When you start to receive guidance, don't shy away from moving towards it. You were given that vision for a reason and you are the one that's supposed to bring it into fruition. Don't question it; just go for it. You might have to go against the grain, but stand confident in your truths.

For instance, people said no one could run a 4-minute mile until the first person did it. Then, other people to did the same. It only takes one person to do it; then others will follow.

The reality is that people will try to discourage you, but you have to stand firm in your beliefs. People are so deep in the abyss of their own negativity that they can't even fathom something working out for somebody else. Also, they can be threaten because of who you are, but that's none of your business. You have to stand ten toes down solid for yourself; knowing that what you want will come at the right time. Even if you feel lost, keep trying things because no one really knows what they're doing either.

Embrace The Variety

Stepping outside of your comfort zone is nerve-wrecking because of the uncertainty. We question whether we have what it takes and wonder where the resources are going to come from, but that is a part of our human experience. As long as we're above ground, we still have time to go after what we want.

Make sure to place your attention on what you do want and when you see other things happening around you, just shift your focus. For instance, if you were cooking a peach cobbler and you were looking for the ingredients in your kitchen. Would you look at the apples in disgust just because they weren't what you needed? Of course not, so apply the same principle to your view of the world.

There is variety in the world because we all have different desires. Never believe that what you want to do is overly saturated. The way you express yourself is going to be different than the next person. Just like walking down the aisles of the grocery store, we have different options for everything like cereals, cheese and meat to name a few. And do you really think one of those other companies shied away from getting their products in the store because other options were available. Of course not, so why should you? That's why you have to stay focused on yourself and allow your authenticity to show.

We need you to share those beautiful gifts. Also, there's no set rules how you can express your gifts. Listen to your intuition and go from there. Believe in yourself wholeheartedly and not waiver from what you know is right for you.

Life is full of milestones and it won't be complete until we take our last breath. As one cycle ends, another one begins. One ending makes way for a new beginning. Never be afraid of something new and remain open because it allows for better experiences.

Perspective Is Key

I know how frustrating it can be to do something for a period of time and not see any results. To be quite honest, you have to be delusional with yourself. You have to start moving like you already have what it is you want to be, do or have in your life. I know it's hard to do when you don't have the experience, but using your imagination can help.

When it comes to dealing with other people, you do want to have a "realistic" approach with them. What I mean is taking people for face value. A lot of times, we do the opposite. We take ourselves for face value and think that what we see isn't good enough, but when it comes to other people, we get delusional and go so deep into these "relationships" that we end up hurting our own feelings. Yes, you may "see" something in someone and think, "We can do X, Y, and Z together," but this isn't going to work if the person isn't even doing anything for themselves.

We have to shift our perspective from other people and turn it back towards ourselves. Whenever we think about ourselves, it needs to be done from the most optimistic outlook. The only person we can control and change is ourselves. So, why not put all that energy back into ourselves.

We are multifaceted and you have to accept when it is time to shift. I used to rely on others to tell me what to do with my life, but that was because I was insecure. Thank God for awareness and healing though. You will know when it's time move on with your life. Trust me. We've all had situations that had an expiration date whether that be a relationship or a job, but we stayed longer than needed. And most times, we suffered more thinking that something would miraculously change. So don't delay what is going to happen whether you want it to or not.

Daily Grace

Remember to extend grace to yourself along this journey. Your output will not always be the same; so give it your best day in and day out. Of course, your best one day is going to look different than another, but we know the difference between someone applying themselves and not.

The goal is to be vivacious, full of life and spry; one way to do this is by creating harmony in our lives. This can be done by having a routine and some structure in our lives. Being prepared in advance for certain tasks, helps you keep energy and time available for tasks that need more attention. I like to use a planner and to-do list to keep me on task. I even use the calendar app on my phone to alert me when it's time to do things write, go to yoga or pilates class and even something simple like wearing my retainer at night.

Also, make it a point to find gratitude for your present day. Does that mean you're going to be filled with joy and laying in fields of flowers everyday? No, but you can find something to be thankful for, even if it's for your breath.

When unpleasant things happen in our lives, we can either make the best of the situation or get caught in a loop of reactions. In addition, I encourage you to feel any emotions that arise while tending to a situation, but that doesn't mean you have to claim it as your own. In the past, when someone asked me how I was feeling; I would respond like, "I'm frustrated." Then, I realized I needed to put some distance between myself and my emotions and started replying instead,"I'm feeling frustrated." Make it a point to acknowledge how you feel, sit with those feelings and release them afterwards.

Strive to do something everyday that makes you feel good. It doesn't have to be something grand either. I know we hear self-care and think we have to go all out like getting a massage and tending to our hair and nails, but that's not the case.

It can be something as simple as walking in nature, taking a bath, watching your favorite movie, or playing some music and dancing in the mirror. The last one is my favorite. I suggest you creating a list of things that make you feel good and adding it your phone. So when life happens, you'll be able to do something to lift your spirits.

Life is meant to be lived; so give your best today while creating even better future moments for yourself.

Special Thanks

Thank you God for your boundless love residing within me.

To my loving husband, thank you for your continuous support and taking my author photo.

To my beautiful children, thank you for being understanding during the writing process.

To my writing mentor Amirah, thank you for your guidance and encouragement to bring this book to life.

To my amazing family and friends, thank you for always rooting for me. I am truly thankful for the outpour of love and support.

www.ingramcontent.com/pod-product-compliance
Lightning Source LLC
Chambersburg PA
CBHW030518130626
46549CB00007B/3051